The Attack on Pearl Harbor

CORNERSTONES OF FREEDOM™

SECOND SERIES

Tom McGowen

Children's Press®
A Division of Scholastic Inc.
New York • Toronto • London • Auckland • Sydney
Mexico City • New Delhi • Hong Kong
Danbury, Connecticut

Photographs© 2002: AP/Wide World Photos: 25 (U.S. Navy), cover top, cover bottom, 6, 7 bottom, 15, 18, 23, 24, 26, 27, 44, 44 top, 45 bottom; Corbis Images: 11, 12, 28, 37 (ACME), 19, 38 (Bettman), 16, 45 center (Museum of Flight), 30 left (U.S. Navy), 13, 17, 21, 40, 41 (UPI), 14, 30 right, 32, 33, 36; U.S. Navy: 3, 4, 7 top, 9, 10, 31, 34, 45 top.

XNR Productions: Map on p. 8

Library of Congress Cataloging-in-Publication Data

McGowen, Tom.
The attack on Pearl Harbor / Tom McGowen.
p. cm. — (Cornerstones of freedom. Second series)

Summary: Explores the relationship between the United States and Japan that led to the surprise attack on Pearl Harbor, Hawaii, in 1941, and to the United States' entry into World War II.
Includes bibliographical references and index.
ISBN 0-516-22586-3
1. Pearl Harbor (Hawaii), Attack on, 1941—Juvenile literature. 2. United States—Foreign relations—Japan. 3. Japan—Foreign relations—United States. [1. Pearl Harbor (Hawaii), Attack on, 1941. 2. World War, 1939-1945—Causes. 3. United States—Foreign relations—Japan. 4. Japan—Foreign relations—United States.] I. Title. II. Series.
D767.92 .M38 2002
940.54'26—dc21

2002001648

Printed in the United States of America.

1 2 3 4 5 6 7 8 9 10 R 11 10 09 08 07 06 05 04 03 02

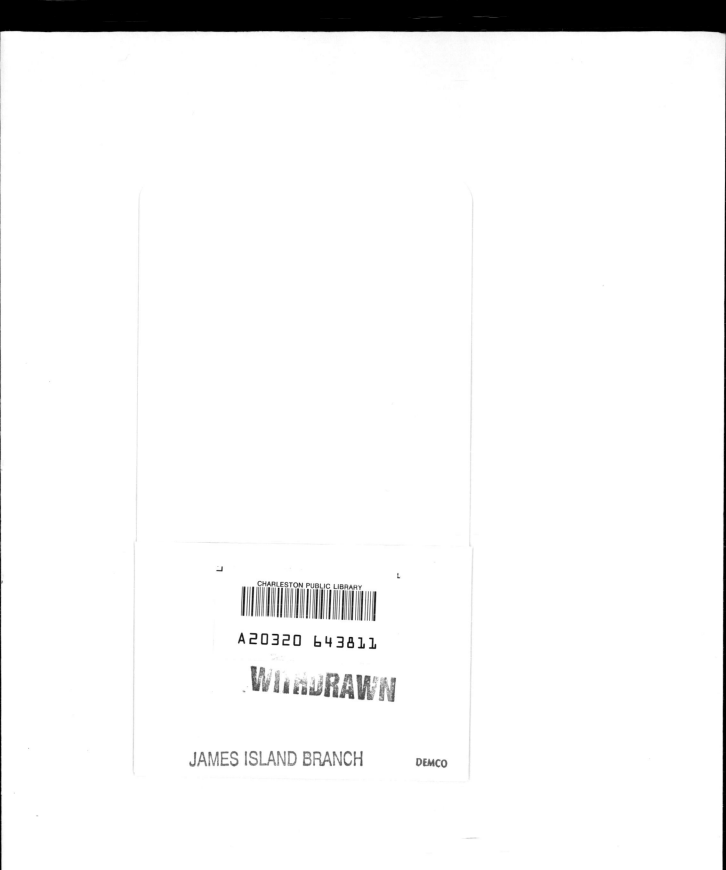

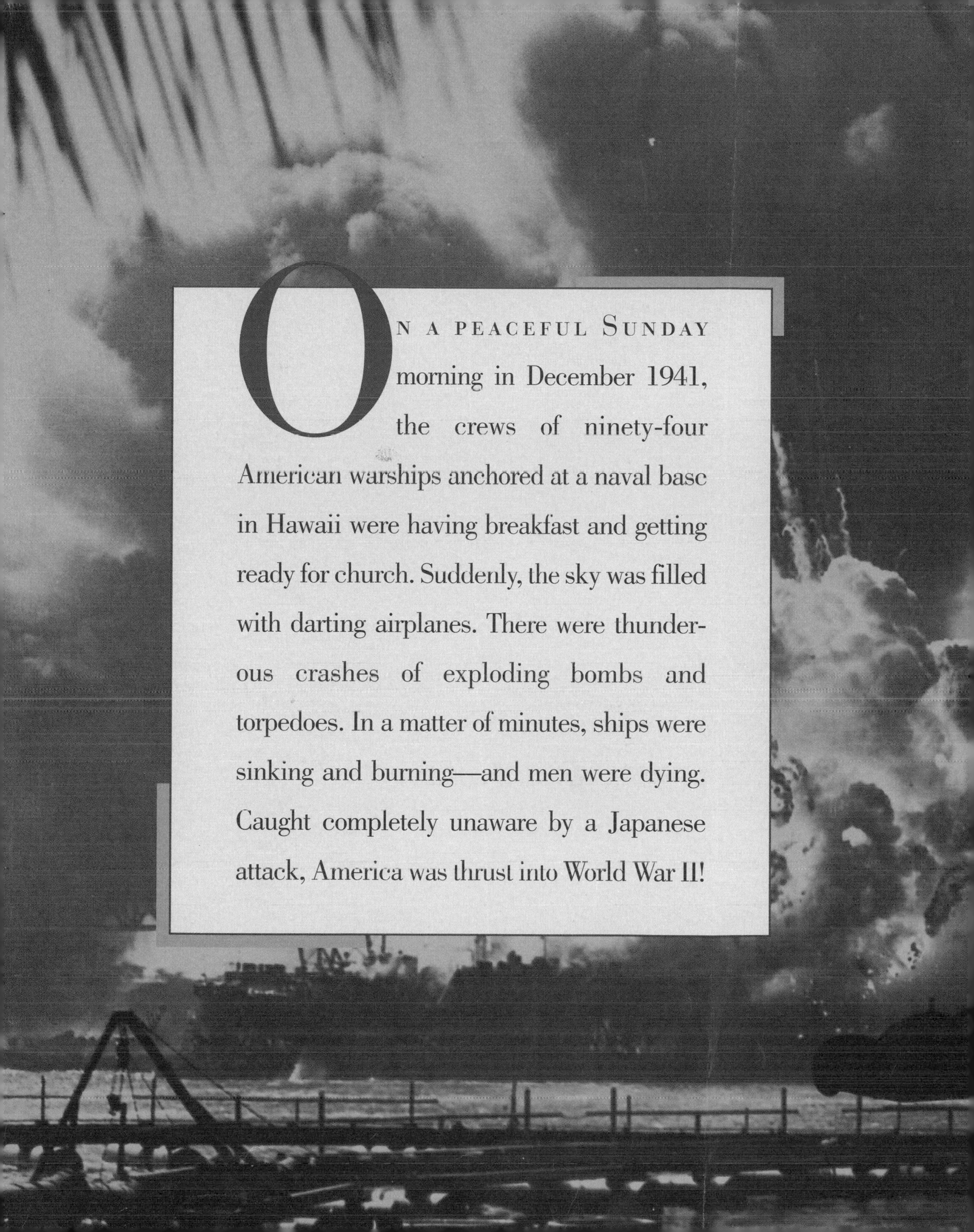

On a peaceful Sunday morning in December 1941, the crews of ninety-four American warships anchored at a naval base in Hawaii were having breakfast and getting ready for church. Suddenly, the sky was filled with darting airplanes. There were thunderous crashes of exploding bombs and torpedoes. In a matter of minutes, ships were sinking and burning—and men were dying. Caught completely unaware by a Japanese attack, America was thrust into World War II!

Onlookers inspect the wreckage left behind after the attack. Smoke can still be seen rising out of the background.

During the first thirty years of the twentieth century relations between the United States and the Empire of Japan were often very unfriendly. Leaders of both nations felt sure that someday there would be war between them.

Japan considered itself to be a poor nation. It had none of the natural resources a modern nation needed—very little coal, very little iron, no oil, no natural gas. Japanese leaders, especially the military leaders, felt they had to gain more land to get some of the things their country needed.

In 1904, Japan began a war with Russia. As a result of that war, Japan took over some Russian territory that was in China. In 1910, it took over Korea, which was then a single country. By declaring war against Germany during World War I (1914–1918) Japan was able to gain some German-owned islands in the Pacific Ocean.

In the 1920s, a group of Japanese Army officers formed a kind of political party. They wanted Japan to become the greatest power in Asia, and they felt that America and other western countries were preventing that. They took power by assassinating several government leaders who were friendly to America. In 1931, they sent an army into China and seized the northernmost part, called Manchuria.

The United States and many other nations condemned this as an act that threatened world peace. The Japanese stayed where they were however, and in 1937 they began a full-scale war, pushing further into China. It was obvious they intended to conquer the country.

In September 1939 World War II began in Europe. Great Britain and France were on one side, and Germany was on the other. By June of 1940, Germany had conquered France. In September, Japanese forces invaded the French colony of French Indochina (now the countries of Vietnam, Laos, and Kampuchea), which had great resources of oil and tin.

The United States government decided to force Japan to stop its **aggression.** American industries had been selling

Japanese soldiers celebrate a victory in China.

Japan oil, scrap metal, and other materials that could be used for warfare, but now the government put a stop to any further sales.

The end of these sales presented a serious problem for Japan. To continue its conquests, it needed these materials. The only other way it could get them was by invading and conquering places that produced them—such as the Dutch East Indies (now called Indonesia), which held rich oil fields. At the same time, Japanese leaders knew such actions would certainly start a war with the United States. They also knew that their country would have no chance against America in a long war because, unlike America, Japan could not produce the huge number of ships, planes, and other weapons needed to fight a war successfully. Therefore, Japan's leaders came to the conclusion that they had to do something to prevent the possibility of a long war.

Japanese Fleet Admiral Isoroku Yamamoto planned the attack on Pearl Harbor.

THE PLAN TO CRIPPLE THE U.S. FLEET

The man who devised a plan to avoid a prolonged war with the U.S. was the commander of the Imperial Japanese naval fleet, Admiral Isoroku Yamamoto. Yamamoto's plan was to launch a giant surprise air raid against the U.S. Navy's fleet in the Pacific Ocean and destroy as many of its battleships as possible.

At that time, battleships were the most important kind of ship in any nation's navy. Armed with ninc to sixteen huge guns, a battleship was basically a floating fort that could stay back out of range of

The U.S. Navy's Pacific Fleet. Planes from the fleet's aircraft carriers fly high above the ships.

Map of the Pearl Harbor attack

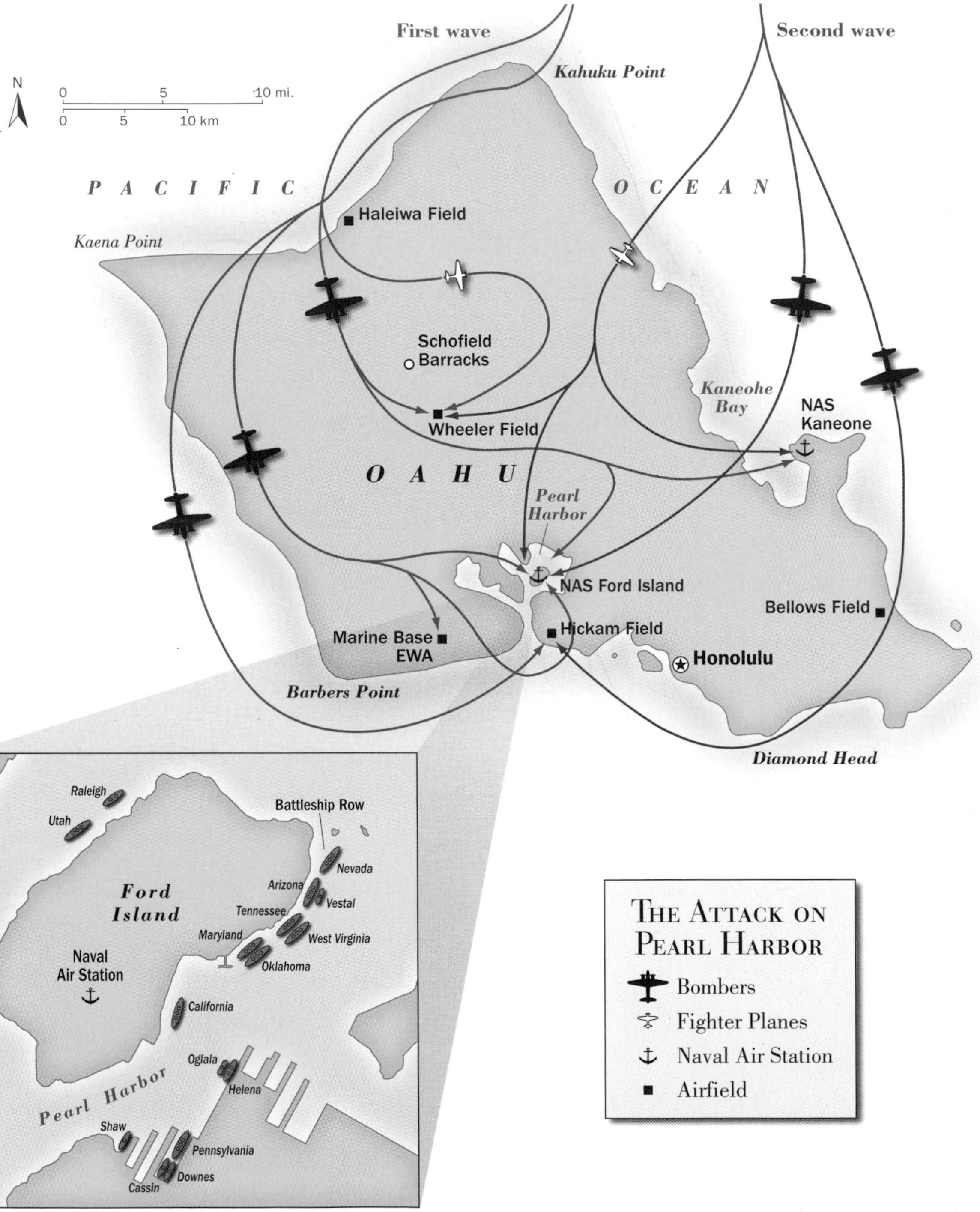

First wave
Second wave
Kahuku Point
N
0 5 10 mi.
0 5 10 km
PACIFIC OCEAN
Haleiwa Field
Kaena Point
Schofield Barracks
Kaneohe Bay
NAS Kaneone
Wheeler Field
OAHU
Pearl Harbor
NAS Ford Island
Bellows Field
Marine Base EWA
Hickam Field
Honolulu
Barbers Point
Diamond Head
Raleigh
Utah
Battleship Row
Nevada
Arizona
Vestal
Tennessee
West Virginia
Maryland
Oklahoma
Ford Island
Naval Air Station
California
Oglala
Helena
Pearl Harbor
Shaw
Pennsylvania
Downes
Cassin
The Attack on Pearl Harbor
Bombers
Fighter Planes
Naval Air Station
Airfield

An aerial view of Battleship Row. This is similar to what the Japanese pilots saw during their attack.

smaller ships with less powerful guns and pound them to pieces with its own gunfire. If a battleship did come in range of enemy guns, its armor, up to 18 inches (46 centimeters) of super-hard steel, would protect it from serious damage. Thus, battleships were the "heavy sluggers" of a navy, and the more battleships a navy had, the more powerful it was considered.

As the 1940s began, the United States had nine battleships in the Pacific Ocean. Japan had ten battleships, and was building an eleventh. Admiral Yamamoto was convinced that if most of America's Pacific battleships could be destroyed, the American government would quickly seek peace and Japan would be free to do as it wanted in Asia.

Pearl Harbor, Hawaii, a 10-mile (16 kilometer) wide **bay** of ocean water, on the southern coast of the Hawaiian island of Oahu, was the U.S. Navy's most important base.

U.S. AND JAPANESE LEADERS AT THE BEGINNING OF THE 1940s

In 1941 the U.S. president was Franklin D. Roosevelt. The ruler of the Japanese Empire was the Emperor Hirohito. However, it was the Japanese prime minister, General Hideki Tojo, and the generals and admirals who actually ran the country.

In the middle of the harbor is Ford Island, which had **piers**—platforms extending from the shore out over the water—on two sides where ships could dock, and an airfield for Navy planes. Through reports gathered from his spies, Admiral Yamamoto knew that every Sunday all American battleships of the Pacific Fleet would be lined up in a double row, known as Battleship Row, along the southeast side of Ford Island. He planned to launch his big attack at Pearl Harbor on Sunday, December 7, 1941.

SECRECY, SURPRISE, TRICKERY!

To make sure the attack would be a complete surprise, Yamamoto decided not to follow the rules of war. At that time, before a nation attacked, it generally presented its

Japanese planners plot out the attack on Pearl Harbor in a wading pool.

Young Japanese pilots in training on a naval air base. Rigorous physical exercise was a major part of their routine.

enemy with an official notice—a message indicating it's intent to wage war. This usually gave the enemy nation a little time to prepare for an attack. Yamamoto's plan was to give the United States notice, but then attack right away so that there would be no time to prepare. This plan was kept very secret. Only the highest officers of the Japanese Navy and a few of Japan's government officials knew about it.

To see if the attack would work, the Japanese Navy high command conducted war games on September 5, 1941. Naval officers representing the forces of each side moved models of ships and planes according to strict rules observed by umpires. During the game, the side representing the American forces was able to sink two of the Japanese carriers. Even so, the outcome of the game indicated the attack could be highly successful. The Japanese Navy decided to go ahead with it.

Japanese aircraft-carrier pilots began to train for the attack, flying over an area that resembled Pearl Harbor and dropping bombs and **torpedoes** on targets representing ships. They also spent hours studying maps and models of the harbor.

The Japanese Navy put together a fleet of six aircraft carriers, two battleships, three cruisers, eight destroyers, and a number of supply ships. On November 26 this fleet set off to carry out the attack on Pearl Harbor. The fleet did everything possible to keep the its movements secret. To keep out of sight of any other vessels, it took a wide, zig-zagging route, starting out in rather dangerous waters well north of most **shipping lanes.** If it did encounter any ships, regardless of whatever nation they belonged to, it was under orders to sink them so they could not report what they had seen. The Japanese fleet kept completely silent, not sending out any radio messages.

The Japanese cruiser Chikuma during its launching ceremony.

Japanese ambassadors, pictured, after a talk with U.S. officials on November 17, 1941—twenty days before the attack on Pearl Harbor

Earlier in the year, two Japanese ambassadors had gone to the United States to talk to American officials about trying to keep peace between the two nations. To prevent the Americans from suspecting that Japan was preparing to attack, Japanese military leaders told the ambassadors to continue discussing peace—but didn't tell them an attack was coming. So even as the Japanese war fleet sailed, these two ambassadors, who didn't know they were part of a trick, were sincerely trying to avoid war.

DRAGONS, CRANES, AND CASTLES

Japanese aircraft carriers had poetic names. The six carriers sending planes to attack Pearl Harbor were the *Hiryu* (Flying Dragon), the *Soryu* (Green Dragon), the *Hokaku* (Soaring Crane), the *Zuikaku* (Happy Crane), the *Kaga* (Increased Joy), and the *Akagi* (Red Castle).

THE AIR WEAPONS OF THE JAPANESE NAVY

The Japanese fleet arrived 270 miles (435 km) off the coast of Oahu in early morning darkness, at about 4:30 A.M., on December 7. Preparations for the attack began immediately. Each carrier started sending planes from its hangar deck up to the flight deck, which served as the runway.

Japanese dive-bombers warm up and get ready to take off for their attack on Pearl Harbor

Japanese aircraft carriers had three kinds of airplanes—attack bombers, dive-bombers, and fighters. All of these planes were propeller-driven. There was no such thing as a jet aircraft yet.

Japan's attack bomber was the Nakajima B5N, which had a three-man crew, made up of a pilot, a navigator-bomber, and a radioman. The radioman was also a gunner, manning a machine gun facing the tail. The B5N could carry a 1,764-pound (800 kilogram) torpedo for attacking ships. The B5N attacked by dropping down to 100 feet (30 meters) or less above the water and flying straight at the ship that was its target. Some distance away it dropped the torpedo, which then sped through the water, propelled by a small engine, toward the ship. The B5N could also carry a one-ton (0.9 metric ton) bomb.

A Japanese bomber goes into its last dive after being hit by Naval antiaircraft fire.

The dive-bomber was the Aichi D3A1. This was a two-seater plane with a pilot in front and a gunner behind, facing toward the tail. The D3A1 was armed with two machine guns in the nose and one in the tail, and could carry a 550-pound (249.5 kg) bomb or two 132-pound (59 kg) bombs. These planes attacked by diving almost straight down at the target, dropping a bomb from a height of several hundred feet, then quickly pulling up out of the dive before the bomb exploded.

EII-142

Japanese Zero fighter in flight. This plane was difficult for the U.S. to fight because it was easy to handle and had great range.

RED "MEATBALLS" ON SILVER WINGS

Japanese aircraft-carrier planes were generally covered with unpainted silvery metal, and had black-painted noses. Painted on the body and wings of their warplanes was a solid red circle, the symbol of Japan. American soldiers and sailors called it a "meatball."

The fighter plane was the Mitsubishi A6M Reisen, which became known to the Americans as a Zero or "Zeke." This plane had a small cannon in each wing and two machine guns on the body, and it could also carry two small bombs. If the ship it was protecting was attacked by enemy planes, it was the fighter planes' job to shoot down those enemy planes before they could do any damage. If their ship was making an attack, the fighters went along with the bombers to defend them from enemy planes. Fighters could also attack ships and targets on land with their machine guns and bombs.

THE ATTACK BEGINS!

Airplanes were not the only weapons used in the attack. The Japanese had built a number of "midget" submarines. These were only 78 and a half feet (24 m) long, carried two torpedoes, and were operated by a two-man crew. Admiral Yamamoto had decided that five of these submarines could slip into Pearl Harbor before the airplane attack began. As soon as the airplanes started to attack, the submarines were to fire their torpedoes into any target they chose.

As the Japanese planes prepared to take off, the weather was not good. There were thick clouds overhead, and the sea was rough. All the ships were pitching and rolling. If this had been a training exercise, it would have been canceled. However, this flight could not be canceled because then Japan's

A Japanese bomber takes off from a carrier.

Ruins of a Japanese two-man sub show the portion rammed by a destroyer and the rippled dents caused by depth charges.

plans would be ruined. The pilots and crew members were strapped into their seats, their plane engines roaring. The carriers turned into the wind and increased their speed so that the push of the wind would help the planes take off.

At exactly 6:00 A.M., planes began rising up from each carrier. A total of fifty fighters went first, followed by fifty B5Ns carrying bombs, then fifty dive-bombers, and finally, forty B5Ns armed with torpedoes. By 6:15 A.M., all 190 planes were headed toward Pearl Harbor.

At about this time the Japanese midget submarines began trying to sneak into Pearl Harbor. At 6:33 A.M. an American patrol plane sighted a midget sub and radioed its location to the U.S. destroyer *Ward,* which was patrolling the entrance of the **channel** that led into Pearl Harbor. The *Ward* raced to the spot and dropped **depth charges**—explosive devices that blow up underwater. The submarine was destroyed. At about 7:00 A.M., another American patrol plane sighted a midget sub and also dropped depth charges to destroy it. Both the *Ward* and the patrol plane quickly sent reports to naval headquarters, but no one paid any attention to them.

THE MINIATURE SUBMARINES

The engines of the mini-subs weren't powerful enough to take the subs very far. So, each mini-sub was clamped on a regular-sized submarine, carried piggyback to its destination, and launched into the water there.

An intact Japanese midget sub, captured during the attack, on display at Pearl Harbor.

AN IMPORTANT DISCOVERY AND A MAJOR MISTAKE

A little after seven o'clock, when the Japanese planes were about 132 miles (211.2 km) from Oahu, they were picked up by a U.S. Army radar station on the island's coast. The soldier watching the screen was astounded to see a huge fuzzy white spot appear, a **blip** that seemed to indicate a large flight of planes heading straight for Oahu. He quickly phoned his commanding officer.

The officer made a serious mistake. He could not imagine that any nation would attack without first declaring war. Having been told that a flight of American bombers was coming from California, he assumed that was what the radar screen was showing. So he told the soldier not to worry.

If that officer had contacted his superiors or if people at naval headquarters had paid attention to the reports from the *Ward* and the patrol plane, someone might have realized that Pearl Harbor was about to be attacked. Someone could have warned the harbor, but instead nothing was done. Thus, forty minutes later, when the Japanese planes came roaring over the coast of Oahu, there was nothing to stop them. The sky over Oahu was clear and sunny, but no American fighter planes were in the air, no American **antiaircraft guns** were firing. The pilot in command of the attack told his radio operator, "Notify all planes to attack." The flight began to spread out, each group of planes heading toward its assigned target. The time was 7:49 A.M.

"TORA, TORA, TORA!"

When the Japanese planes reached Oahu, they sent a radio message back to their ships: "Tora, tora, tora" ("Tiger, tiger, tiger"). This was a code word telling their fleet commander that the Americans had been caught by surprise.

Seven American battleships were in Battleship Row alongside Ford Island. American battleships were named after states, and the first ship in the row was the *Nevada*. The *Arizona* was next, with a little repair ship named the *Vestal* beside it. Then came the *Tennessee* and the *West Virginia*, side by side, followed by the *Maryland* and the *Oklahoma*, also side by side. The *California* was at the end, by itself. An eighth battleship, the *Pennsylvania*, was in dry dock (a waterless repair area) nearby.

Firefighters on the U.S.S. *Nevada* try to put out fires during the attack.

★ ★ ★ ★

Also in the harbor were eighty-six other U.S. warships. Eight of these were cruisers—smaller, faster battleships—and twenty-nine were destroyers—small, fast ships used mainly for fighting submarines. The remainder were submarines, **minelayers, minesweepers,** repair ships, and fuel tankers.

THE ATTACK ON BATTLESHIP ROW

At just about 7:55 A.M., sailors on a number of these ships suddenly noticed the gleaming shapes of airplanes rushing toward them out of the sky. A line of twelve attack bombers swooped down low over the water, straight at the battleships. Dive-bombers came with them, higher overhead. To most of the sailors the first moments of the attack were puzzling. The air was suddenly swarming with fast-moving planes, and most men thought it must be a "drill," a fake air raid by the Army Air Force to put them on alert.

But then, there was a sudden explosion and a burst of smoke, as a bomb struck on Ford Island. Moments later, with shattering explosions, three torpedoes blew holes in the side of the *Oklahoma*. As water rushed in, the ship began to lean to one side.

Only a minute later, the *Arizona* was hit with five torpedoes. At about the same time, the *West Virginia* was hit by six, perhaps seven, torpedoes and then by two bombs. The torpedo explosions ripped the ship open and one of the bombs started a fire. The *West Virginia* slowly settled down

Water spouts up in the background as a ship is hit by a torpedo.

into the harbor. However, the top deck was still above water, and crewmen were firing at the Japanese planes with every antiaircraft gun that still worked.

A single plane roared at the cruiser *Raleigh* and launched its torpedo, which blew a hole in the *Raleigh*'s side. The *Raleigh* began to take in water and lean over. While some crewmen worked to prevent the ship from sinking, others fought off attacking planes with antiaircraft fire. The *Raleigh* was bombed and **strafed,** but managed to shoot down five of its attackers and to stay afloat.

The *Maryland* was protected from torpedoes by the *Oklahoma,* which had now turned over and was lying upside down alongside it. However, the *Maryland* was hit by two bombs. Although the bombs killed four men and wounded fourteen, they did very little damage to the ship.

CRUISER NAMES

U.S. cruisers were named after cities. The *Raleigh* was named for the capital city of North Carolina. Another cruiser, the *Helena,* named for the capital of Montana, was damaged by a torpedo in the attack on Pearl Harbor.

Antiaircraft gunners of the U.S. Army who fired on Japanese planes during the attack on Pearl Harbor

After fuel tanks in the ships have been shattered, flaming oil spreads over the water at Pearl Harbor. Barely visible through the smoke are a damaged U.S. battleship and the capsized U.S.S. *Oklahoma.*

The *Nevada,* at the front of the row, managed to have all its antiaircraft guns operating by 8:00 A.M., when some torpedo planes attacked it. The gunners shot one plane down, and several other planes veered off. At 8:03, one aircraft managed to launch a torpedo that tore a hole in the *Nevada*'s side. Moments later, one bomb and then another exploded on the battleship's deck, causing structural damage and casualties. Rather than allow the ship to just sit and be a target, the *Nevada*'s commanding officer ordered the ship to get under way and head for the harbor entrance and the open sea. The *Nevada* began to move through the oily, burning water and the thick clouds of smoke.

BURNING WATER!

Explosions on the ships sent burning fuel oil flying in all directions. Since oil floats on water, the flaming oil spread out on top of the water, turning much of Pearl Harbor into a sea of flame.

THE ATTACK ON THE AIRFIELDS

Even as Pearl Harbor was shuddering from the thunder of bomb and torpedo explosions, every U.S. Army, Navy, and Marine Corps airfield on Oahu was under attack by Japanese fighters and dive-bombers. The bomb dropped on Ford Island at 7:55 missed its target, but a bomb dropped a few moments later blew a hangar to pieces. Most of the planes at the airfield were out in the open, in small groups on the field. The planes had been kept in plain sight purposely, to guard against **sabotage,** but this made things much easier for the Japanese bombers. Bombs began to explode among the groups of planes, flinging them broken and burning in all directions. Within just a few minutes, thirty-three planes were destroyed.

HOW AMERICANS LEARNED THEY WERE AT WAR

Although it was morning in Hawaii when the Japanese attacked, it was afternoon in America. Many people were listening to radio broadcasts of football games or to their favorite Sunday programs. Suddenly, announcers broke in to proclaim that America was at war!

At 7:58, with bombs still falling, an officer on Ford Island managed to order all radio operators to send out the message:

AIR RAID PEARL HARBOR.
THIS IS NOT DRILL!

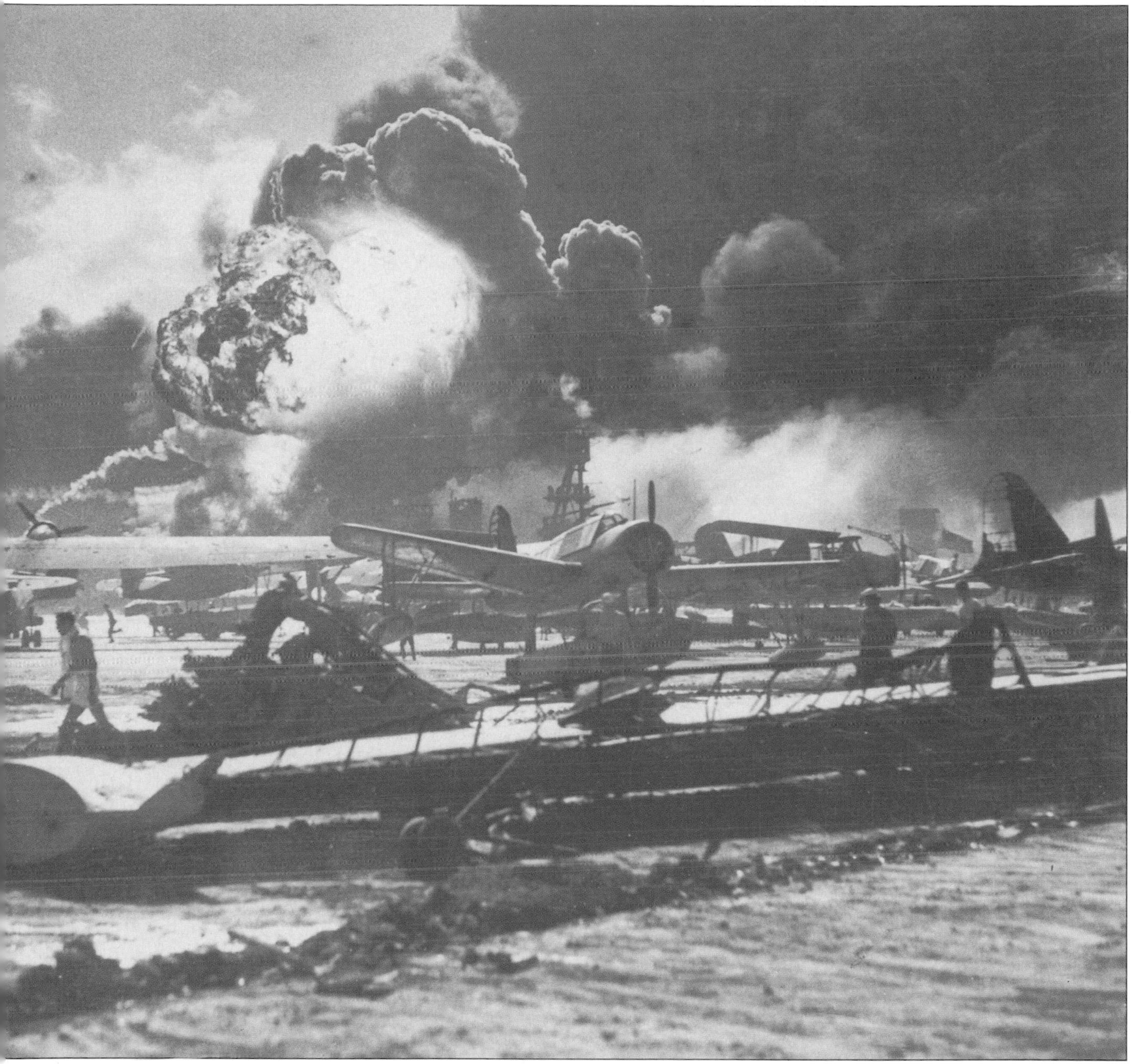

Debris covers the ground and smoke fills the sky as planes are bombed on an airfield during the attack.

Hickam Field, a main target for the Japanese, was turned to rubble during the attack.

When this message was received at radio stations in the United States, the reaction was shock. It meant that America was at war! This was a tremendous surprise because the Japanese official notice had not yet been given to the U.S. government.

Fifty-one American planes were lined up in the open at the U.S. Army Air Force base of Hickam Field. Japanese dive-bombers dropped bombs on buildings and hangars, and then zoomed over the field machine-gunning the rows of planes and anyone near them. Thirty-five men were killed and many injured when a bomb exploded in the **mess hall,** where soldiers and airmen were having breakfast.

Forty-nine planes were on the field of the U.S. Marine Corps Air Station at Ewa. Suddenly twenty-one Japanese fighter planes were swooping over the field. They machine-gunned the lined-up planes with **incendiary bullets** and explosive bullets, destroying twenty-seven of them.

At 8:02 twenty-five dive-bombers roared over the U.S. Army Air Force base of Wheeler Field. With bombs and machine-gun fire they destroyed most of the planes on the field. A squadron of dive-bombers also struck the U.S. Naval Air Station at Kanehoe, where thirty-three big Catalina patrol planes were kept. The bombers destroyed all but three planes.

MORE BATTLESHIPS MEET DISASTER

At 8:05 A.M. the battleship *California* in Pearl Harbor was hit by two torpedoes, which blew holes in its side. Water flooded in, and the ship began to tilt to the side. The crew tried to take measures to prevent the ship from sinking. Despite every effort, the *California* eventually settled nose-first into the mud on the harbor's bottom.

At 8:08 the *Arizona* was hit by a bomb from a dive-bomber. The bomb exploded in an ammunition compartment holding about 1,600 pounds (726 kg) of gunpowder. The resulting explosion was so powerful that it actually lifted the *Arizona* out of the water, broke it in two, and knocked men off the decks of nearby ships. A mangled, flaming wreck, the *Arizona* sank straight down into the harbor, taking over 1,100 of its crew down with it.

The *Tennessee*, anchored next to the *West Virginia,* was hit with two bombs. It was also showered with chunks of metal and burning powder and oil from the *Arizona* explosion,

Wreckage of the U.S.S. *Arizona,* most of which sank to the bottom of the harbor. Today, the memorial at Pearl Harbor rests over the remains of the ship.

USS ARIZONA MEMORIAL

Fireboat crews battle flames on the U.S.S. *West Virginia.*

which started fires. While some of the *Tennessee*'s crew fought the fires, other crews fired antiaircraft shots at the Japanese planes buzzing overhead.

At about 8:10 a Japanese midget submarine managed to get into the harbor, and surfaced. The U.S. destroyer *Helm,* which was heading for the harbor entrance, saw the sub almost directly in its path and sped up to ram it. The

Japanese bombers fly through black puffs of smoke from antiaircraft fire.

submarine was badly damaged but managed to submerge. A short time later it came up again and ran aground on the beach. One crewman was dead, and the other was taken prisoner.

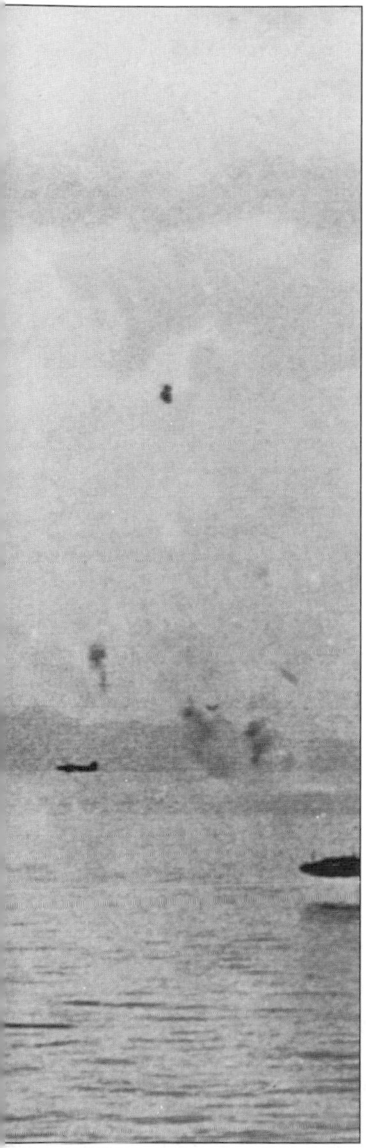

At 8:30 another midget sub was sighted in the harbor. The U.S. destroyer *Monaghan,* making its way toward the harbor entrance, swerved toward it. The sub fired a torpedo at the *Monaghan,* but missed. At top speed, the *Monaghan* sped through the water and rammed the sub, slamming into it and dropping two depth charges. By 8:40 the midget sub was completely destroyed.

The first wave of Japanese aircraft had now finished its job and turned to head back to its carriers. The second wave—consisting of 170 planes, 50 NK5s with bombs, 80 dive-bombers, and 40 fighters—came roaring over the harbor at 8:50. There were no American fighter planes in the air to fight back because most of the American aircraft were lying wrecked on the fields that the Japanese dive-bombers had attacked. However, antiaircraft guns were now in action all over the harbor. They opened up with a storm of machine-gun bullets, and black puffs of smoke from shell bursts appeared in the air.

Wrecked warships litter the water. The U.S.S. *Cassin* and the U.S.S. *Downes* lie in dry dock. Behind them is the U.S.S. *Pennsylvania.* The U.S.S. *Helena* sits behind and to the left of the crane.

THE ATTACK RAGES ON!

The second wave of Japanese planes was looking for ships that hadn't been hit by the first wave. The ship that drew their attention was the *Nevada,* the only battleship that was moving and seemed to be all right. The Japanese pilots knew it was heading for the entrance to the harbor, and if they could sink it, its wreckage would block any other ship from being able to get out of the harbor. Dive-bombers headed for the *Nevada* like a swarm of angry bees. Three bombs made hits, tearing the upper deck open and wrecking everything on it. The *Nevada* managed to move away from the harbor entrance, leaving it open, but eventually took on so much water that it had to be beached (run aground) to keep from sinking.

Because the *Pennsylvania* was out of the water in dry dock, torpedo bombers of the first wave hadn't been able to reach it. But now Japanese dive-bombers quickly went after it. At 9:07 A.M., one managed to hit it with a bomb that exploded on the upper deck, killing eighteen men and wounding thirty. Otherwise, the *Pennsylvania* was undamaged and kept up steady antiaircraft fire at its attackers.

However, bombs aimed at the *Pennsylvania* caused trouble for the destroyers *Cassin, Downes,* and *Shaw,* which were also in dry dock nearby. A bomb hit the *Shaw,* blowing its front end off in a thunderous explosion. Another bomb hit the dock between the *Cassin* and the *Downes* and set both ships afire. As the crews tried to fight the fires they were machine-gunned by fighter planes and were unable to keep the fires from spreading. Eventually, the flames caused explosions in ammunition compartments. By 9:30 both ships were battered wrecks.

* * * *

At about 10:00 A.M., the cruiser *St. Louis* was just at the end of the channel leading out of Pearl Harbor into the open sea. Suddenly, two torpedoes fired from a Japanese midget submarine just outside the channel came streaking toward it. Both missed, but the *St. Louis* opened up with its guns and apparently sank the sub, which was never seen again. The five midget submarines had all been destroyed without causing any damage to the U.S. ships.

...we here highly resolve that these dead shall not have died in vain...
REMEMBER DEC. 7th!

THE BATTLE ENDS

The battle was now over. The second Japanese attack flight was heading back to its carriers. The Japanese had lost twenty-nine airplanes and all five midget submarines. The United States had lost four battleships and one was beached. A number of other ships had been sunk or damaged. In addition, 261 army, navy, and marine corps airplanes had been destroyed or damaged. A total of 2,335 servicemen had been killed and 1,143 wounded. Sixty-eight civilian workers had been killed and thirty-five injured.

Pearl Harbor was the worst defeat suffered by the United States in World War II in terms of ships and aircraft lost all at one time. However, in a way it was a victory. The attack on Pearl Harbor enraged Americans, who called it a sneak

WE'LL ALWAYS
REMEMBER PEARL HARBOR
Words and Music by
ALFRED BRYAN
WILLIE RASKIN
and
GERALD MARKS
MILLS MUSIC

Advertisement for the song "We'll Always Remember Pearl Harbor," written by Alfred Bryan, Willie Raskin, and Gerald Marks

WAR SWEEPS THE WORLD

On December 8, the day after the attack, the United States and Great Britain declared war on Japan. On December 11, Japan's allies, Germany and Italy, which were already at war with Great Britain and Russia, declared war on the United States.

attack. Japan did not actually give the United States official notice that it was going to war until thirty-five minutes after the attack began. The attack pulled America together, making people determined to defeat Japan at any cost. In the

A group of men enlist in the United States Army Air Corps. They will be assigned to the 99th Pursuit Squadron at Chanute Field, Illinois. This is the first time the U.S. Army Air Corps had opened its enlistment to African Americans.

days after the Pearl Harbor attack, men flocked by the millions to join the armed forces. America's new slogan "Remember Pearl Harbor" quickly appeared on posters, signboards, and banners displayed in windows of stores, taverns, barber shops, and business offices throughout the country. A popular song titled "Let's Remember Pearl Harbor" was frequently played on radio programs throughout the war.

The sunken battleships *West Virginia* and *California,* and the beached *Nevada,* were raised and repaired. They took part in the rest of the war. The *Oklahoma* was raised, but was so badly damaged that it had to be scrapped. In 1962 a memorial was built over the wreckage of the *Arizona,* which still lies at the bottom of Pearl Harbor with the remains of all the men who went down with it. The ship is officially still in the U.S. Navy, and the U.S. flag is raised over the memorial every morning and lowered every evening, just as flags are raised and lowered every day on all U.S. Navy ships and all U.S. Navy and U.S. Army bases.

Pearl Harbor Memorial, built over the wreckage of the battleship U.S.S. *Arizona,* off the island of Oahu.

Glossary

aggression—an attack or invasion

antiaircraft guns—cannons or machine guns that can fire projectiles high enough into the sky to destroy enemy aircraft

bay—an area of seawater partly enclosed by land but with a channel leading out into the sea

blip—a fuzzy white spot on a radar screen indicating a distant object or objects

channel—a long, narrow, strip of water

depth charges—explosive devices that blow up underwater

incendiary bullets—bullets filled with a chemical that can cause any flammable object it hits to burn

mess hall—a building at a military base where food is cooked and served to soldiers and airmen. The U.S. Navy refers to such a building for sailors as a "Chow hall."

minelayers—small ships that drop mines (floating explosive devices) into the water

minesweepers—small ships that have the duty of destroying floating mines

piers—platforms extending from shore out over water, to which a ship or boat can be tied

sabotage—the destruction of weapons, vehicles, supplies, or war materials by enemy agents

shipping lanes—areas of the ocean in constant use by ships of many nations as "paths" from one place to another

strafed—people or objects on the ground or on the deck of a ship machine-gunned by an airplane

torpedoes—explosive missiles that move through water, propelled by a small engine at the rear

Timeline: Pearl Harbor

Sunday Morning, December 7, 1941

4:30
Japanese attack fleet arrives 270 miles from Pearl Harbor.

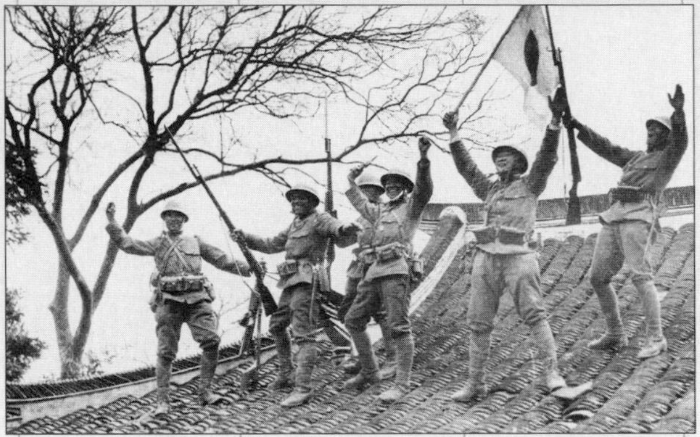

6:00
First attack wave begins taking off from Japanese aircraft carriers.

6:33
Japanese midget submarine sighted at entrance to Pearl Harbor. The U.S. destroyer *Ward* destroys it with depth charges.

7:00
U.S. patrol plane sights another midget submarine outside Pearl Harbor and destroys it with depth charges.

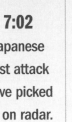

7:02
Japanese first attack wave picked up on radar.

7:40
Japanese first attack wave reaches Oahu.

7:49
Commander of Japanese first attack wave orders attack to begin.

7:55
The *Oklahoma* torpedoed; turns over and sinks. The cruiser *Raleigh* torpedoed. Japanese dive-bombers attack naval airfield on Ford Island, destroying thirty-three planes.

7:56
The *West Virginia* torpedoed; settles on harbor bottom with only top deck above water.

EII-142

8:02
Twenty-five Japanese dive-bombers attack the U.S. Army Air Force base of Wheeler Field, destroying and damaging sixty-two airplanes.

8:03
The *Nevada* hit by a torpedo and two bombs and then begins an attempt to leave the harbor.

8:05
The *California* torpedoed and begins to sink.

8:08
The *Arizona* hit by a bomb causing an explosion in an ammunition locker. The *Arizona* sinks nine minutes later.

8:10
The U.S. destroyer *Helm* rams and damages a Japanese midget submarine. One of the crewmen dies, and the other is later captured.

8:40
The U.S. destroyer *Monaghan* rams and sinks a Japanese midget submarine.

8:50
Japanese second attack wave reaches Oahu.

9:07
The *Pennsylvania* hit by a bomb.

9:30
The U.S. destroyers *Cassin* and *Downes* badly damaged by fire and explosions.

10:00
The U.S. cruiser *St. Louis* destroys fifth Japanese midget submarine with gunfire.

To Find Out More

BOOKS

Hasday, Judy L., *Pearl Harbor.* Broomall, PA: Chelsea House, 1991.

Hatt, Christine.*World War II: 1939-45.* Danbury, CT: Franklin Watts, 2001.

McGowen, Tom, *Carrier War: Aircraft Carriers in World War II.* Breckenridge, CO: Twenty-First Century Books, 2001.

Tames, Richard, *Pearl Harbor: The U.S. Enters World War II.* Portsmouth, NH: Heinemann Library, 2001.

ONLINE SITES

Naval Station Pearl Harbor
http://www.pearlharbor.navy.mil/

Pearl Harbor Attack—1941
http://history.acusd.edu/gen/WW2Timeline/Prelude23.html

Pearl Harbor Remembered
http://www.execpc.com/~dschaaf/mainmenu.html

Index

Bold numbers indicate illustrations.

About the Author

Tom McGowen is a children's book author with a special interest in military history. He has written fourteen previous books in this area. His most recent book in the Cornerstones of Freedom Series is *The Battle of Midway.* Fourteen years old at the time of the attack on Pearl Harbor, he served in the U.S. Navy during the final year of World War II. Author of fifty-six fiction and non-fiction books for young readers, he has received the Children's Reading Round Table Annual Award for Outstanding Contributions to the Field of Children's Literature.